MW00929083

Don't hesitate to make this book your own.

Use bookmarks to mark important sections, underscore key points with a marker, and inscribe your thoughts directly onto the pages.

Keep revisiting these laws regularly. By doing so, you're reinforcing their significance, ensuring that my past mistakes don't become your future ones.

Law 1

FOCUS ON YOU, PEOPLE COME AND GO.

Law 2

IF YOU DON'T
CONTROL YOUR MIND,
SOMEONE ELSE WILL.

Law 3

SOMETIMES,
THE THINGS THAT
BREAK YOUR HEART END UP
FIXING YOUR VISION.

Law 4

LONELINESS IS THE PRICE YOU PAY WHEN YOU START TO IMPROVE YOURSELF.

Law 5

BE PROUD,
YOU SURVIVED THE DAYS
YOU THOUGHT YOU
COULDN'T.

Law 6

NOT EVERYONE WILL LIKE YOU, THAT'S LIFE.

Law 7

STOP TELLING
PEOPLE EVERYTHING.
MOST PEOPLE DON'T CARE,
AND SOME SECRETLY
WANT YOU TO FAIL.

Law 8

BE KIND,
BUT DON'T LET PEOPLE
USE YOU.

Law 9

IT IS BETTER TO BE
HATED FOR WHAT YOU ARE
THAN TO BE LOVED FOR
SOMETHING YOU
ARE NOT.

Law 10

DON'T GO BROKE
TRYING TO IMPRESS
BROKE PEOPLE.

Law 11

STAY AWAY
FROM PEOPLE WHO
MAKE YOU FEEL LONELY.
NO COMPANY IS BETTER
THAN A BAD COMPANY.

Law 12

MAKE PEACE WITH
YOUR PAST SO IT WON'T
SCREW UP THE PRESENT.

Law 13

DON'T COMPARE
YOUR LIFE TO OTHERS.
YOU HAVE NO IDEA WHAT
THEIR JOURNEY IS
ALL ABOUT.

Law 14

NEVER UNDERESTIMATE THE POWER OF STUPID PEOPLE.

Law 15

NO ONE IS GOING
TO FIGURE OUT YOUR LIFE.
IT'S YOUR RESPONSIBILITY.

Law 16

SOMETIMES YOU WIN, SOMETIMES YOU LEARN.

Law 17

IF NOBODY HELPS YOU
– DO IT ALONE.

Law 18

TAKE YOUR
FINANCIAL LIFE SERIOUSLY.
MONEY IS A DEFENSE TO A LOT
OF CHALLENGES.

Law 19

BE SELFISH
WITH YOUR TIME.
A LOT OF PEOPLE DON'T
DESERVE IT.

Law 20

WHAT OTHER PEOPLE THINK OF YOU IS NONE OF YOUR BUSINESS.

Law 21

YOU CAN'T GO BACK
AND CHANGE THE BEGINNING,
BUT YOU CAN START WHERE
YOU ARE AND CHANGE
THE ENDING.

Law 22

BEING ALONE
GIVES US AN OPPORTUNITY
TO RECONNECT WITH
OURSELVES.

Law 23

SOMETIMES
YOU NEED TO STOP
SEEING THE GOOD IN PEOPLE
AND START SEEING WHAT
THEY SHOW YOU.

Law 24

DON'T PRETEND TO
BE BETTER THAN YOU ARE.
LIVE LIFE AT YOUR
OWN PACE.

Law 25

LIFE IS TOO SHORT
TO WASTE TIME HATING
ANYONE.

Law 26

YOUR DEEPEST,
DARKEST MOMENT
MAY BE THE BEST THING THAT
EVER HAPPENS TO YOU.

Law 27

ENVY IS A WASTE OF TIME.
YOU ALREADY HAVE
ALL YOU NEED.

Law 28

IF YOU DON'T ASK,
YOU DON'T GET.

Law 29

DO UNTO OTHERS
AS YOU WOULD HAVE THEM
DO UNTO YOU.

Law 30

IF YOU TELL THE TRUTH,
YOU DON'T HAVE TO
REMEMBER ANYTHING.

Law 31

LIFE ISN'T FAIR,
BUT IT'S STILL GOOD.

Law 32

HE WHO IS NOT COURAGEOUS ENOUGH TO TAKE RISKS WILL ACCOMPLISH NOTHING IN LIFE.

Law 33

DON'T TRUST WORDS.
TRUST ACTIONS.

DO YOURSELF A FAVOR,
GET RICH — LIFE GETS EASIER
WITH MONEY, NOT TIME.

Law 35

IF YOU CAN SURVIVE
YOUR OWN THOUGHTS,
YOU CAN SURVIVE ANYTHING.

Law 36

IF THEY DON'T
APPRECIATE YOU,
THEY DON'T DESERVE YOU.

Law 37

LEARN TO HEAL
WITHOUT VENTING
TO EVERYONE.

Law 38

TO AVOID DISAPPOINTMENT, EXPECT NOTHING FROM NOBODY.

Law 39

EVERYTHING COMES
TO YOU AT THE RIGHT TIME.
BE PATIENT AND TRUST
THE PROCESS.

Law 40

FAILURE IS A BRUISE, NOT A TATTOO.

Law 41

AVOID GOSSIP AT ALL COSTS.
IT'S POISON TO YOUR MIND.

Law 42

THE ROOT OF ALL SUFFERING IS ATTACHMENT.

Law 43

TIME ALWAYS EXPOSES WHAT YOU TRULY MEAN TO SOMEONE.

Law 44

STRESS IS TEMPORARY,
BUT THE LESSONS YOU LEARN
FROM IT CAN LAST
A LIFETIME.

Law 45

IF SOMEONE
IS TRYING TO BRING
YOU DOWN, THEY ARE
ALREADY BELOW YOU.

Law 46

MONEY ISN'T
EVERYTHING IN LIFE,
BUT IT CAN HELP YOU SOLVE
A LOT OF PROBLEMS.

Law 47

NO MATTER HOW
SMART, SUCCESSFUL AND
GOOD-LOOKING YOU ARE,
NOBODY LIKES ARROGANCE.

HUMILITY IS EVERYTHING.

Law 48

DON'T REGRET
HAVING A GOOD HEART,
ALL GOOD THINGS COME BACK
AND MULTIPLY.

Law 49

DON'T FEEL GUILTY
FOR DOING WHAT'S
BEST FOR YOU.

Law 50

CHOOSE
YOUR FRIENDS WISELY.
THE FASTEST WAY TO BECOME
BETTER IS TO SURROUND
YOURSELF WITH BETTER
PEOPLE.

Law 51

BE LOYAL OR STAY SINGLE,
THAT'S SIMPLE.

Law 52

EXPECT NOTHING,
APPRECIATE EVERYTHING.
BE GRATEFUL FOR THE LITTLE
THINGS IN YOUR LIFE TO
FIND INNER PEACE.

Law 53

DO YOUR BEST
AND TRUST THE PROCESS.
THE HARDER YOU WORK,
THE LUCKIER YOU
WILL GET.

Law 54

NEVER TAKE
ANYTHING PERSONALLY.
WHAT OTHERS SAY AND DO
IS A PROJECTION OF THEIR
OWN REALITY.

Law 55

BE FORGIVING.
BE UNDERSTANDING.
BUT DO NOT BE A FOOL.

Law 56

NEVER SAY
'MAYBE' IF YOU WANT
TO SAY *'NO'*.

Law 57

WHEN SOMEONE
SHOWS YOU WHO THEY ARE,
BELIEVE THEM THE FIRST TIME.

Law 58

YOUR SELF-RESPECT
HAS TO BE STRONGER THAN
YOUR FEELINGS.

Law 59

DON'T LET
SUCCESS GO TO YOUR HEAD,
DON'T LET FAILURE GO
TO YOUR HEART.

Law 60

THE BEST WAY
TO RESPECT YOURSELF
IS TO DISCIPLINE YOURSELF.

Law 67

IF YOU ARE A GIVER,
REMEMBER TO LEARN YOUR
LIMITS BECAUSE THE TAKERS
DON'T HAVE ANY.

Law 62

DON'T WASTE YOUR
TIME WITH EXPLANATIONS:
PEOPLE ONLY HEAR WHAT
THEY WANT TO HEAR.

Law 63

ACCEPT CRITICISM,
BUT NEVER ACCEPT
DISRESPECT.

Law 64

NEVER GIVE UP
ON SOMETHING YOU REALLY
WANT, IT'S DIFFICULT TO WAIT,
BUT IT'S MORE DIFFICULT
TO REGRET.

Law 65

WHEN YOU ARE ANGRY, STAY SILENT.

Law 66

YOU HAVE THREE
CHOICES IN LIFE — YOU CAN
WATCH THINGS HAPPEN,
MAKE THINGS HAPPEN,
OR WONDER WHAT THE HELL
HAPPENED.

Law 67

STAY STRONG,
EVEN WHEN THINGS
BEGIN TO FALL APART,
STAY STRONG.

Law 68

YOU'RE BEING
JUDGED NO MATTER WHAT,
SO BE WHO YOU WANT
TO BE.

Law 69

YOU DON'T HAVE
TO WIN EVERY ARGUMENT.
AGREE TO DISAGREE.

NO REGRETS,
JUST LESSONS.
NO WORRIES,
JUST ACCEPTANCE.
NO EXPECTATIONS,
JUST GRATITUDE.
LIFE IS TOO SHORT.

THE CALMER YOU ARE,
THE CLEARER YOU THINK.

Law 72

THE MORE YOU ARE
INTERESTED IN OTHERS,
THE MORE INTERESTING
THEY FIND YOU.

TO BE INTERESTING,
BE INTERESTED.

Law 73

IF YOU ARE NOT
FALLING DOWN OCCASIONALLY
YOU ARE JUST COASTING.

HATRED IS A CURSE
THAT DOES NOT AFFECT
THE HATED, IT ONLY POISONS
THE HATER.

RELEASE A GRUDGE
AS IF IT WAS POISON.

Law 75

WE SUFFER MORE
IN IMAGINATION THAN
IN REALITY.

Law 76

PEOPLE CHANGE.
LOVE HURTS.
FRIENDS LEAVE.
THINGS GO WRONG.
BUT REMEMBER THAT
LIFE GOES ON.

Law 77

LEARN TO
SAY '*NO*' WITHOUT
EXPLAINING YOURSELF.

Law 78

BE A GOOD PERSON,
BUT DON'T WASTE YOUR TIME
PROVING IT.

Law 79

NEVER TELL YOUR
FRIENDS YOUR PLANS,
STOP PUTTING TOO MUCH
TRUST IN THEM.

DON'T LET ANYONE
KNOW WHAT YOU'RE
DOING UNTIL IT'S
DONE.

Law 80

IF YOU
WANT TO BE TRUSTED,
BE HONEST.

Law 81

THE ONLY PERSON
THAT CARES ABOUT YOUR
HOPES AND DREAMS IS YOU.

THE ONLY PERSON
THAT IS GOING TO MAKE
THEM HAPPEN IS YOU.

Law 82

FORGET WHAT HURT YOU,
BUT NEVER FORGET WHAT IT
TAUGHT YOU.

MASTERING OTHERS
IS STRENGTH.

MASTERING YOURSELF
IS TRUE POWER.

Law 84

EVEN THE NICEST PEOPLE HAVE THEIR LIMITS.

Law 85

YOUR DIRECTION IS MORE IMPORTANT THAN YOUR SPEED.

Law 86

CONTROL YOUR THOUGHTS,
OR YOUR THOUGHTS
WILL CONTROL
YOU.

Law 87

DON'T OVERSHARE.
PRIVACY IS POWER.

Law 88

DON'T MAKE
A PERMANENT DECISION
BASED ON TEMPORARY
EMOTIONS.

Law 89

TO BE THE BEST, YOU MUST BE ABLE TO HANDLE THE WORST.

Law 90

AS LONG AS YOU ARE ALIVE,
NO OBSTACLE IS PERMANENT.

Law 91

YOU LEARN
NOTHING FROM LIFE
IF YOU THINK YOU'RE RIGHT
ALL THE TIME.

Law 92

STAY PATIENT.
THE BEST THINGS HAPPEN
UNEXPECTEDLY.

Law 93

NEVER REGRET
A DAY IN YOUR LIFE:
GOOD DAYS GIVE HAPPINESS,
BAD DAYS GIVE EXPERIENCE,
WORST DAYS GIVE LESSONS,
AND BEST DAYS GIVE
MEMORIES.

Law 94

LIFE IS A ONE-TIME OFFER, USE IT WELL.

Law 95

BE YOURSELF.
PEOPLE DON'T HAVE
TO LIKE YOU, AND YOU DON'T
HAVE TO CARE.

Law 96

FREE YOURSELF
FROM SOCIETY'S ADVICE,
MOST OF THEM HAVE NO IDEA
OF WHAT THEY'RE DOING.

Law 97

FIRST,
IT HURTS,
THEN IT
MAKES YOU
STRONGER.

Law 98

NORMALIZE
WALKING SOME PATHS ALONE
BECAUSE GOALS ARE
PERSONAL.

Law 99

THE FAMILY YOU CREATE IS MORE IMPORTANT THAN THE FAMILY YOU COME FROM.

Law 100

LIFE IS SHORT, LIVE IT.

LOVE IS RARE, GRAB IT.

ANGER IS BAD, DUMP IT.

FEAR IS AWFUL, FACE IT.

MEMORIES ARE SWEET,

CHERISH THEM.

And here we are, at the end of this journey.

As you close this book, keep in mind that each day is a new chance to apply these laws, to learn, to grow, and to change. Don't let past mistakes define you. Instead, use them as stepping stones toward your own transformation.

You have the power to create a life you love, so why wait?

As the last page turns, I hope these laws have inspired you, challenged you, and maybe even scared you a little. That's a good thing. It means you're ready to face your own reality and make it better.

Remember, it's never too late to rewrite your life script. With these 100 laws of life, you now have a roadmap not to screw up your life like I did. Embrace them, learn from them, and watch as your life blossoms into something extraordinary.

June 28, 2023